28 PIXELS OF FEBRUARY

POETRIES BLEEDS INK

AVINASH KUMAR SINGH

ISBN 979-888591719-3

Contents

Contents

Contents

Preface

Every one knows how important February is for love and love life. February meant for celebrating every moment of love just because of one beautiful day called valentine's day .

Love adore itself on this day . Everyone has a valentine in their life like friends , any family members or your love partner . All you need to celebrate this day with them .

Usually this book defines and discover the hidden love in you and explore it to your loved ones .

You don't need to feel complicated with this term love .

Love is easy if it is well defined in you . Love is the most powerful bond in any relationship .

This book covers the highs and lows of the same love .

" 28 pixels of February " will be a shield to the bond between you and your love .

You can gift this book to them to show your real affection towards them .

Thank you!

Acknowledgements

The book of love is written for every love stuffs that surrounds us . The bond between external and internal of every person is tied with self believe and self love .

No matter you're strong enough to hold yourself in this world of self love , but in this life sometimes their is a need of third hand which can pull you from dreadful situations . When your both hands are hurt to recover you from that phase you need someone to take you back.

Some relationships are good but broken . You need to heal them with your love and care . This book teaches you about 28 days of February , you can love your love to regain your love in your love

.

You can relate to these poems and find how much deep you're in love .

Happy reading !

Prologue

Each poems will hit you in different phase of love .

The book is compiled with my love , each word in each line of the poems will effect your thoughts and affects the love of your life .

Read the poems in eve or morning when you feel free from every work and busy world .

Read with your love , to discover the busy love between both of you .

Happy love !

QUOTE

Love is simple if calladores you more than texts.

1. TEXTS

We spend every minutes in texts,
yet the talks feel incomplete .
We have good memories which reflects ,
each phase of love that is complete.
The texts are important ,
meaningful ,
and crazy to read about .
The Goosebumps in cosy ears,
when you call me love aloud .
All I need is you along with me
my eyes are quite naughty ,
they ask your reflections to see .

QUOTE

When your hairs are heavy , I wrap it around my presence.

2. WET HAIRS

I feel ,

every moment when I see you,

your hairs are wet and are dark .

It's covering up my healthy desires,

It turns the moment

in my heart for quite.

It doesn't care,

of the day or night.

I pulled you to me,

wrapped the part of hair.

Around my face , to calm the beats for while .

Eyes are drained with love

and lips with pure smile .

QUOTE

My heart bleeds in love of your name , this in only a line .

You already defeated me in this love game cause you are mine .

3. GAME OF LOVE

Hey !

I can survive without your air

Cause I love you in your presence and absence

Hey !

I'm loser in the game of love

Look , you won me already.

You have your reward.

You have my love.

You can play the game once again.

You have control ,

over this play and pause

I love you for infinity

There's a reason ,

cause you love me for no cause .

QUOTE

I spent restless number of nights , yet it doesn't mean without you ,

your love , your anger and crazyfights.

4. DESIRES

It's cold without you ,
Blanket don't face your warmth
I'm compiling myself
for your desires .
Warmth and you
Can't get the imagination off
Where are you now ,
come soon please ,
I need to love you
with no ease.

QUOTE

Chocolates tastes less sweet when our kiss last minutes long.

5. MINUTES

Wait !
Hold on !
Grab me , pull me close
Now that's ok .
Love me from this distance .
Kiss me
Get some deep ,
Now hold it for minutes
That's too short .
Can't we turn time slow ,
Be mine , let's play
The game of high and low .

QUOTE

The lyrics of love penetrate my feelings for you . Hearing you feels exactly like same .

6. HEAR YOU !

I can't get the words
Would you spell it out
Love !
Stop that's sweet
and cute , should I believe
The voice exists
Which can make my heart ,
turns me off endure.
I want to hear you
Yeah you !

QUOTE

Darkness doesn't turns me erotic for you but you .

7. QUITE EROTIC

Your hands are dramatic

They act dramatically .

Like no guilt

They have not seduced

me for you.

Actually me in you ,

We are close , not in thoughts

Not even in thesepure words .

You see

Yourself in my arms ,

Limbs crossed and chest slides in sweat .

QUOTE

A rose crafts my feeling for you and strengthen our bond .

8. THE RED AND ROSE

The Red and rose

Sweet as it shows

You pluck it from garden

Look at me

From our memories

Thorns and problems

Blood and difficulties

Bandage and belief

Suck and erase

Temporary and not permanent .

QUOTE

Each time I'm on knees shows how sudden I fall in love with you.

9. NOT A PROPOSAL

Hey it's not a proposal
It's a call
Call for being mine
If you can't , it's fine
Maybe there's some
hidden , block my love to you .
It's prestigious ,
Art which needs an artist eyes .

QUOTE

Love is funny because it laughs over it's own terms and conditions.

10. TERMS AND CONDITIONS

Okay ! Not so tough
You need to recall
Your memories every time
You feel it's enough
You feel yourself
You're lacking your patience
You are unable to be your best
Love her by every means
You know !
That actually mean .

QUOTE

Love is a drama , and these dramas are real.

11. YOU CAN'T

You can't
Yes !
You can't
But what
I can't
You can't
Make your love drama
even against love karma
You can't bleed yourself
Hiding from your love
Calling it's fake
And that's all
You can't .

QUOTE

Hugs are temporary which affects permanently.

12. HUGS AND BELIEF

Hugs and belief
Short but relief
It's temporary
But lasts permanent
Not a big deal
In this love department .
You get your rhymes
I should get her
Love in hugs
Erase your bugs .

QUOTE

Hey aren't we are magicians ! We can see the reality behind fake emoji.

13. EMOZI

Some smiles
Some hugs
Few kisses
And some tears
All are emotions
Maybe necessary
And sign of our love
Usually that feels perfect
We are magicians
We can read eyes
Feel the pain that lies.

QUOTE

If love is fake , call it hate because love is pure with nothing

negative attached with it.

14. FAKE LOVE

Love isn't fake
It can be funny
Can be romantic
Can be anger
Can be in long distance
You can't spell fake with it
Call it hate
Call if it's like same
You know it's tough
To find pure love
But necessary.

QUOTE

You are my path to the easy love .

15. EASY LOVE

Love isn't same for all
You travel through night alone
You're close on texts
Or with a call on phone
Look you can love from distance
The bond between both of you
Is yet strong .
You can feel how precious will be your meet
Days or months after you will be
In most comfortable arms
All you need is patience
A little wait
That trims the terrific problems
With very ease .

QUOTE

Your presence counts my happiness.

16. PRESENCE

Presence ,
Of your love and you
In my life
Means a lot
Like a sentence ends in dot .
A flower needs a pot
All that's depend
Shows your presence
Rain drops and my skin
Like Your touch
That turns me crazy about you .
All are not just an imagination
We will make it true
Let's become quite phenomenal.
Love in red and dissolve as blue .

QUOTE

Your presents represents state of your excitement .

A way you share your love and of course only to me .

17. PRESENTS

Hey ! You brought one more gift for me
Now I can't wait to see this beautiful .
Let's hold time
Let's see with no boundaries
How long happiness lasts
You're excited
To see the most precious smile
You ever desired of
Okay ! Let's turn off these thoughts
Focus on the box
Tied with ribbon in heart shaped
Wrap in red cover
Unwrap the wrap
Can't wait more to see the beauty
Hey ! You got me sneakers
My fav one , white and classical
Tears rolled down , but it's normal.

QUOTE

Your call heals and I'm happiest with you what I exactly feel .

18. CALLS

My phone rings
I looked at the time
I make my way to the table
It's crucial maybe
You was there
This was not your time
You never called me on same before
Maybe it was normal
But your silence denied it to no more .
Hey! Aren't you're ok
What happened ?
She's determined to her words
Said not at all
Why dear ? What's stopping you to be happy ?
What's making you wet in tears ?
I need you now
Please come close in hurry
Hold me in your arms
Give me your warmth
I need a lap to count my feelings
I need a shoulder to rely my emotions .
I'm making the things possible to happen
Come soon until it turn worse .

Phone rings again
This time again there was she
Coming soon dear wait some parts .
She laughed ! Hey Mr Hallucination
You're missing me badly again .
Come to the street next to your house
The dogs are creepy and cat says meow
I'm standing from a couple of minutes
I got your favourite pizza
Come soon at take me to your home
Come on do it in hurry !
Call ends
Hey my illusion !
What you will pretend ?

QUOTE

Hey be my valentine ! I will love from ninetill you be mine.

19. MY VALENTINE

Valentine

My valentine

You can't get over

Until you be mine

I make this day for you

Special for every second

You can't get enough time to

Look at your long nails

Straighten your hairs

Or colour your lips

All you can do is …look at me

From ease distance

That seems comfortable

We will go out for a date

Have a beautiful dinner in night

We can chill out in clubs

Or enjoy the lake beautiful sight

There's lie your happiness

With me no matter what's exactly the place is

I feel your love in these vibes

And you can count the stars

To define how cool exactly the view is .

QUOTE

Black and white , together looks the beautiful and all right .

20. COLOURS IN ME AND YOU

Colours

In me and you

Black is your beautiful

White shows my view

We are together magicians

We show that black and white do not contradict

Actually they're pair of each other .

We show our bond

Which bleeds in bloody red

Colours shows the true love

We are different and so we love .

QUOTE

We go deep in each but extent is yet out of reach .

21. LUST

We have limits
Each time get kind
Kind to get sexually one
Where our bodies meet
And so our feelings
We doesn't get out of that line
That's out of reach for now
Lust is our feeling
Erotic immerse us in it anyhow
We have emotions
We erase distance like the same
We got a shape for the love game .

QUOTE

Love is hidden in your mind . It's you who stop to get it to your heart .

22. LOVE : MIND TO HEART

Love is also a situation
In which you have to get in
A journey from mind to heart
Love lies in your mind
What exactly you have to discover
Through your heart
Maybe sometimes you get hurt
and that makes you cry
A little bit shy
That shows you're strongin love
How you gave hundred in your try .

QUOTE

Songs in love acts as immune to feelings.

23. SONGS

The way it felt
You can now get lyrics
It's worthy and mean
To your every clicks
You go hassle free
You need no suggestions
All you think made for you
You believe in your creations
Songs the beautiful tunes
Make you best even from worse .

QUOTE

Love is endless with no start and no end . You can feel yourself trapped
in somewhere between .

24. LOVE TRAP

Love is trap
In somewhere between
From no begin and undefined end
You feel yourself in between
Of that trap
While you travel in your life journey
That cause you no hurt
But a little confused
That seems blur quite
Even in sparks and night
You need kind of clear eyes
A vision that makes your way
All clear through .

QUOTE

Love is reasonless . If trying to find one , love because they love you for no cause .

25. CAUSE OF LOVE

Love cause

she don't love you for any cause

Be reasonless

Make her satisfied

Love her in every play pause

Speak the truth

Present her your care

Don't seek ease in it

That's too complicated

Solve this complications

With ease

Remember in love you're too young .

QUOTE

Love can't be creepy as people.

26. CREEPY LOVE

No way
You can't say it
You can't call love creepy
Wait
Maybe you watched people
Quite creepy
Maybe you had lose someone
With the same follow up
Yet you can't blame these things
You need to know the best of this
Love isn't creepy at all
Creepy things don't make you fall .

QUOTE

Love doesn't happens like you see on screens . It's more than that actually .

27. LOVE AND SCREENS

You say

Love is blind

It don't see age or other discrimination

It's a power of authority

To cross every limitation

You never thought beautiful for that

You always look for the negatives

And foolish act .

You thought love is like

How screen shows us

How people talk about it

They are damn wrong

Just feel about it

You everytime think how to prove it wrong

Love is worthy

That required to be earned

You can't chop the green without instruments

Love conveys everything not only about sentiments .

QUOTE

You're enough for your love ....all you need is a little change .

28. YOU

"write anything that's suits this blank best".

Thank You !

Love seems enough and is .

Thank you!